The Advent of Planet Martyr and Other Literary Works

An Innovative Social Commentary

By

Veronica N. Chapman

1663 LIBERTY DRIVE, SUITE 200
BLOOMINGTON, INDIANA 47403
(800) 839-8640
WWW.AUTHORHOUSE.COM

First published by AuthorHouse 03/12/05

ISBN: 1-4208-0358-1 (sc)

Library of Congress Control Number: 2004097837

Printed in the United States of America
Bloomington, Indiana

This book is printed on acid-free paper.

In Loving Memory of Donald T. Walker

Table of Contents

Foreward

There is something about stepping outside one's reality that makes one a better, wiser person. At least this is one of the many lessons I learned while living and studying abroad. Removing myself from the United States, I was able to better understand my position in "my country" and the global position of those who look like me. I am African-American. I prefer to say Black because "African" is too broad a description.

There are two significant events that occurred while I was abroad in the fall of 2001. The Twin Towers tumbled and my cousin, Donald T. Walker was killed. These two events made me furious with humanity. The vilification of Muslims that followed September 11, 2001, and the intentional, slow, but certain demise of the Black community in the United States of America, made me realize that one is not truly human until he or she can surmount what I call the "barriers to humanity." Barriers such as; language, race, socio-economic status, national borders, flags, avarice, and ignorance, have fomented the acceptance of primitive ideologies and resorts.

One of the many attributes that distinguish humans from other animals is that God blessed humans with the ability to think and reason, and accomplish great things through Him. There is a supposed myth alleging that we only use ten percent of our brain. Considering the present state of humanity, I choose to take this myth as fact. Doing so allows me to remain optimistic, hoping that we will one day live up to our potential. Unfortunately, these Berlin Wall - like barriers to humanity still reign. It is imperative that we strive to dismantle these barriers so we can stop impeding our growth, behaving more like cavemen than progressive humans. If we fail to do so, we shall have to prepare for, "The Advent of Planet Martyr," when we will only be animals, aliens to someone else!

De Mon Point De Vue
(Les Poèmes)

Journal Entry
(Let's be real!)

Let's be real!

No one in power wants to share.

Yes, one purpose of business is to minimize expenses,

however business will be conducted as usual, at the expense of:

DEBITS	CREDITS
(+) the poor	(-) CAPITALISM
(+) the sick	
(+) the hungry	
(+) family structure	
(+) education	
(+) morality	
(+) oneself	
(+) minorities	

LIFO!
(Last In First Out!)

Thinking Out Loud
(D'Afrique)

WOULD

I

BUY

A

DIAMOND

IF

VISIONS

OF

MAIMED

AFRICANS

REFLECTED

OFF

EACH

CARAT

?

News Flash
(Waiting to Exhale)

This just in…

A murder committed…

(GASP!)

In a few minutes

a description of the defendant.

A new front passes through the nation, west coast to east.

And it echoes…

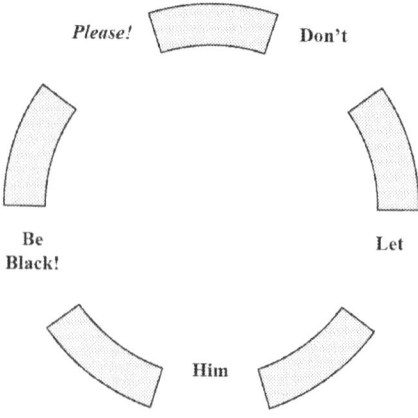

Please! Don't

Be Black! Let

Him

The defendant Tom White…

Exhale… (Shoop Shoop)

Bereavement

(For the African in "African-American")

Today I bathe in black,
And I cry tears that could overwhelm black holes.
I am down…

Mourning a loss yet to be discovered, and presently,
yet to be defined.

African in "African-American," where art thou?
Shall I be left to claim what this country has made of you?
What you are now is an aftermath,

The result of fierce and relentless oppression,
self-hatred, and self-destruction.
Your true identity has not been revealed.

It remains hidden,
Hidden behind the years
Only to tease us with the beat of each and every drum.

African in "African-American," I long to know you.
I miss you,
Even though I know you are a part of me.

A part of me…
Some say we have been mixed and assimilated so much,
We wouldn't recognize you if we saw you.

But I felt you in Cuba,
And I liked your touch…
It was reassuring and empowering.

African in "African-American,"
Here you are being pimped and mocked.
Here, your people pretend to "bling-bling"
All while making money for the oppressor,

Without a tinge of reparations in the distance.

And so,
Today I bathe in black once more,
And I cry tears that could overwhelm black holes.
I am down…

Mourning a loss yet to be discovered,
And presently,
Yet to be defined.

Time For A Touch-Up

Weeks go by smooth,

like my roots,

when I leave my Black hair salon.

And I return home

to stroll through the quiet and cold suburban streets,

where I'm the only one.

Memories of double-dutch and porches full of friends

have been replaced with lacrosse

and children consuming liquor to no end.

Playing rhythmic hand games on the corner

and dancing in the streets…

None of that here,

no one can keep a beat!

Judgments before I speak

All formed from watching TV

Impressed with my ability to think!

Like we are incapable!

Yes I am well spoken,

and no, I won't be your token!

The ONE you had in your house!

Like the gray hairs that come with age,

I am burdened with so much rage.

I must re-straighten my roots…

It's time for a touch-up.

Malcolm X Revisited

I miss Malcolm X.

I miss his words.

I miss his wisdom.

I miss his courage.

I miss him.

I crave his direction.

I often visit with him,

Captivated by each and every word he says.

And I listen attentively to him,

As I turn the pages.

I pray his words are infectious,

And that those who read and hear them are diagnosed with the desire

To do something!

Symptoms should include:

Headaches for knowledge,

And major irritation due to injustice.

RX, keep your prescriptions!

I want this epidemic to spread like butter…

Whipped and battered,

Like us.

Idolatry

When one depicts the devil
It should no longer be red and evil, clenching a pitchfork.
But calm, decorative, and passive,
Effortlessly attaining followers that will sacrifice all for it

The devil is composed while relaxing in our pockets.

Yet, for the devil man steals
For it man kills
For it man pimps
For it man oppresses
For it man stresses

But how does this devil assume command over the common
individual?
This devil can't even talk!

This devil is ink!
This devil is codes!
This devil is an emblem!
This devil is paper!

This devil is money.

So the next time one portrays the devil,
One should draw paper with ink,
Adding an emblem and security codes,
Then when people laugh at this portrayal,
It will be at themselves, whom they are laughing,

Too embarrassed to openly acknowledge their idol!

American...*I Think*

(A True Story)

Native I am not,
so I'm not American.
Whatever that is.

The last time I checked,
Amerigo V. is the reason for
North, South, and Central
"America"

But I'm not a United Statesman either.
For no one is.

It took me twenty years to find that out,
in a classroom
in France.

"Where are you from?"

Asks the French professor to his three "American"
students.
Italy, says one, Ireland, another
United States I say, the only "Afro-American."

"No, originally," the professor says, confused by my
response.

I thought...
Don't look at me like that!
Because I don't know!

I wanted to say,
ask your neighbors!
The Portuguese, the Spanish, the Dutch, then <u>you</u> tell me!

Don't you remember the Middle Passage?

I don't think they issued receipts
in anticipation of any returns or vessel credit.

We didn't come with instructions, warranties, or stickers
that read "Made in Nigeria", "Ghana", or "Angola."

So professeur please accept,
Je ne sais pas, as my response.

Don't condemn me for the iniquities of others.
I don't want a failing grade for this group project!

The Scarlet Letters,
M.I.N.O.R.I.T.Y.

(Ode to "The Majority")

You are the m.i.n.o.r.i.t.y!
Don't do me no favors!
Your favors are laced!
Leaving lasting, even fatal repercussions that diminish the
mind and spirit!
You are the m.i.n.o.r.i.t.y!
You have achieved nothing alone!
Ethics, a word you can not define.
Terrorists! Who? Shut yo' mouth!
Before the skeletons come tumbling down!
Don't vilify me!
You have been the source of endless tragedy!
Justice shall prevail…

Black Daddy, Who Should We Beat?

Black Daddy says,

"I beat you because I love you!"

Smack!

Black Daddy says,

"If I don't they'll kill you!"

Smack!

"Do you want to wind up like...

"Amadou Diallo?"

Smack!

"Nathaniel Jones?"

Smack!

"Paul Childs?"

Smack!

"Abner Louima?"

Smack!

"Emmett Till?"

Smack!

"Your cousin?"

Smack!

Black Daddy departs for work stressed, and tired,

from preparing his black son for life in the land of the free.

He races for the mighty dictator

who is green with a large white face,

only to be halted by land sharks,

the predators that be.

Black Daddy remains *calm*!

Protocol, both hands on the wheel.

Don't fidget, don't blink!

Best not breathe or else!

Or else what?

Must we repeat the smacks?

Oh, Black Daddy!

Who should we beat?

Esperanza

Espero el día en que todas las personas sean iguales.
Espero…

Espero el momento en que no haya ninguna forma de
racismo.
Espero…

Espero el día en que todos respeten las varias culturas que
existen en el mundo.
Espero…

Espero el momento en que la familia sea más importante
que el dinero.
Espero…

Espero el día en que los líderes de los países del mundo
sepan que ellos no tienen el poder, sino que es Dios que lo
tiene.
Espero…

Y después de que muchos años pasen, alguien todavía
estará esperando.
Espero.

Esperanza
(Hope)

I await the day when all people are equal.
I'm waiting…

I await the moment when there is no form of racism.
I'm waiting…

I await the day when all people respect the various cultures
that exist in the world.
I'm waiting…

I await the moment when family is more important than
money.
I'm waiting…

I await the day when the world leaders know that they
don't have power, but that it's God who has it.
I'm waiting…

And after many years pass, someone will still be waiting…
I hope.

MarsEx

Why worry about life on Mars when we could care less
about life here on Earth?

Spending billions to roam the red planet while ignoring
our grounds

red with the blood of

Iraqi children

Massacred Rwandans

innocent young soldiers

and the ghetto stream

While ignoring

the homeless

the hungry

Haiti.

There are dogs with better healthcare than my mother.

Well, maybe not mine,

but no one really cares about anyone else's plight

so I personalized it, letting it hit home

like the Twin Towers.

But did it really have to come to that?

No!

If to whom much is given, much is expected,

This country owes much more than the balance of the U.S. deficit.

And has more to worry about than,

Who J-Lo is dating,

Botox shots,

"And oh, which Starbucks flavor should I have today?

Caramel Macchiato or Mocha Latte?"

Oh, how low can we go,

until the U.S. is synonymous with shallow?

Because all we care about is US.

So who really gives a damn about life on Mars?

When we're still battling AIDS, Avarice, Genocide, and SARS?

Extremist I may be, but nothing's more extreme than the ills of society.

Question everything!

Unfinished Business
(Timothy's Testimony)

"As we were walking towards the roof, the door to the stairwell opened.

Then a shot rang out…"

R.I.P.
Timothy Stansbury Jr.
January 24, 2004
Louis Armstrong Houses, Ground Floor, Brooklyn, NY

It could have been my little brother.

Ancestors Inc.

Cast of Characters

Nekia Williams - Quincy's mother
Quincy Williams (age eight)
Quincy Williams - Main character/Teenager
Terrence - Teenager/High Achiever/Classmate
Student One - Teenager/Classmate
Teresa - Teenager/Classmate
Thomas - Teenager/Quincy's friend/Classmate
Lamont - Teenager/Quincy's friend/Classmate
Student Two - Teenager/Classmate
Sista Clark - Church mother
Sista Williams - Church mother
Sista Johnson - Church mother
Aletha Turner - Vendor/Ancestor
Church Choir
Ms. Moreno - Spanish Teacher
Santiago - Nekia's love interest
Waiter
Slave Master
"E-Drums" Store Manager
Male slave
African Dancer
Robert Bogle – Ancestor/Dancer
James Forten – Ancestor/Dancer
James Boon – Ancestor/Dancer
Dr. Martin Luther King Jr. – Ancestor/Dancer
Marcus Garvey – Ancestor/Dancer
Huey Newton – Ancestor/Dancer
Malcolm X – Ancestor/Dancer
Madame C.J. Walker – Ancestor/Dancer

Act I

Scene 1: Stage left: Early morning on a southern
plantation
Stage right: Early morning in Washington, D.C.
Scene 2: Early afternoon at church
Scene 3: The Williams' living room
Scene 4: School classroom

Act II

Act I

Scene 1

Lights up. Music is playing: "Come Ye"... sung by Nina Simone. The following all happens simultaneously.

Stage Right:

A woman is selling fruits and vegetables. After a day of hard work the woman counts her money. After counting her money the woman becomes ecstatic. She suddenly changes to a reverent position and begins to pray over the money collected. After counting her money, the saleswoman exits stage right and resurfaces at stage left where a male slave is working.

Center Stage:

An African woman is dancing behind a screen. Her dance is one that evokes pain and sorrow for the Africans that were sold into slavery.

Stage Left:

There is a male slave working in the field moving to the rhythm of the music.

The saleswoman summons the slave master and gives him some money. He counts the money after which the slave master releases the slave.

The slave master leaves. The man and woman embrace in the absence of the slave master. They then kneel in prayer facing Heaven.

Blackout.

Scene 2

Lights up. The scene is NEKIA'S husband's funeral in a church sanctuary. The church choir is singing "Goin' Up Yonder" as the lights come up. The family of the deceased is sitting in the front of the church. NEKIA is sitting in the front pew in silence; she appears to still be in shock. QUINCY (age eight) is sitting alongside her trying to gain her attention. After the choir has finished singing, "Goin' Up Yonder" the pianist begins to play the recessional. The pallbearers exit with the casket followed by the family of the deceased. The three mothers of the church are the last persons to exit the sanctuary. They begin to straighten up the sanctuary after everyone has left the funeral.

SISTA CLARK: That poor child, left all alone to care for her son.

SISTA WILLIAMS: Well you know Sista Clark; I heard that she's been caring for him by herself ever since that chile was born.

SISTA JOHNSON: Sista Williams what are you talking about? *(Convicting)* You always know everyone else's business. *(Slyly stated)* Though I'd be lyin' if I said I don't like hearing it!

SISTA WILLIAMS: Well one good thing is that her husband was paid so she won't have to worry about money. Unfortunately her husband was a workaholic. He didn't spend much time with her at all, and even less time with their son!

SISTA CLARK: Well sistas all we can do is take it to God in prayer. Talking has never done anything for anyone. We must pray that her son takes the right paths in life and that his mama has the strength to do all that must be done. It's so hard to raise a child alone.

SISTA WILLIAMS: You are so right Sista Clark!

SISTA JOHNSON: Lord help her!

The women exit the sanctuary as the light darkens.
Blackout.

Scene 3

Lights Up. Eight years have passed. The scene is the living room of the Williams household. NEKIA is reading on the couch while waiting for QUINCY to return. The room is filled with pictures of her and her husband. QUINCY'S school pictures also garnish the room. NEKIA begins to look at her watch and wonders why QUINCY has not returned home from school. QUINCY finally enters the house. He's fairly tall with a medium build.

NEKIA: *(agitated)* Q, where have you been?

QUINCY: Out with my friends. How are you? *(He kisses NEKIA on her forehead.)*

NEKIA: With which friends? And why are you getting home so late?

QUINCY: You know my friends, Thomas and Lamont. We were chillin' downtown after school.

NEKIA: I remember telling you that I'm not fond of them. They seem to have no direction. What could you possibly gain from hanging around with them? Now Terrence down the street, he's on the ball! His mother told me that he just won some Black Enterprise young entrepreneur award. You need to surround yourself with kids who are doing things and going places!

QUINCY: Mama he is so wack! All he does is read and study. I would never be seen with him!

NEKIA: Whatever, Quincy! I know one thing; you better spend more time with your books instead of those delinquent friends of yours. Your father always had goals and aspirations. It's about time you get some!

QUINCY: Yeah, well look where it got him, six feet under!

NEKIA: Quincy, how dare you! *(Stated slowly and sternly.)*

NEKIA looks at QUINCY with a look of disgust and disappointment and retreats to her room. QUINCY is left alone pensive and apologetic.

Blackout.

Scene 4

The curtain rises. Ibrahim Ferrer's music is heard in the background. We are in QUINCY'S Spanish class. His teacher, MS. MORENO, is at the blackboard.

MS. MORENO: Today, we are going to learn about a brilliant Afro-Cuban writer, Nicolás Guillen. Does anyone know what he's famous for?

STUDENT ONE: Didn't he create the "Son" poem?

MS. MORENO: And let's see…. *(She takes a look at the roll.)* Terrence, what is el poema son?

TERRENCE: El poema son is a poem in which Guillen mixed the Cuban son, music enriched with African characteristics, with the typical verses of a Spanish poem.

(THOMAS and LAMONT make mocking faces towards TERRENCE)

MS. MORENO: *(She begins to hand out a sheet of paper to each student.)* Well, today we are going to read one of Don Guillen's famous poems. Now, who wants to begin reading?

TERESA: I would like to Ms. Moreno!

MS. MORENO: Okay Teresa, always begin with the title!

TERESA begins to read. She struggles somewhat with the Spanish pronunciation.

TERESA: Negro Bembon…

While TERESA is reading, THOMAS, LAMONT, and QUINCY are talking in the back of the room. They are being very disruptive.

MS. MORENO: Teresa dear, stop for one moment. *(She looks toward the back of the classroom, towards LAMONT, THOMAS & QUINCY. She speaks to them sternly)* Excuse me gentlemen! You are here to learn! I will not have any other disturbances!

(The boys look at her blankly.)

MS. MORENO: You may continue Teresa.

TERESA: *(TERESA continues to read with trepidation.) The boys continue to talk. MS. MORENO notices the disturbance and is extremely agitated. TERESA looks up from her paper and looks at MS. MORENO, who is looking at the boys.*

MS. MORENO: *(Still looking at the boys who are still talking.) (Sternly)* Gentlemen! I have warned you, now I must send you to the principal's office!

MS. MORENO escorts THOMAS, LAMONT, and QUINCY to the principal's office as the curtain closes.

Blackout.
End of Act 1

Act II

Scene 1

As the lights come up NEKIA is out to lunch with SANTIAGO, a co-worker. It is obvious that they are attracted to each other. They are talking somewhat close to one another, sitting at opposite ends of the table. The scene begins with NEKIA'S laughter.

SANTIAGO: Well Ms. Nekia, enough about work. Tell me a little about yourself.

NEKIA: Well, what would you like to know?

SANTIAGO: You mentioned that you have a son. Tell me about him.

NEKIA: Quincy... *(She pauses and sighs.)* Quincy is a brilliant young man. The problem is that he doesn't want anyone to know it. He thinks it is okay to be average. *(She's gradually getting upset. SANTIAGO notices this.)* He hangs out with some wayward children, and the other day at school... *(SANTIAGO interrupts.)*

SANTIAGO: Whoa! Whoa! I can see that the little man has you stressed! Well calm down, we'll talk more about you, and take care of Quincy later. *(He smiles.)*

NEKIA'S cellular phone rings.

NEKIA: Hello... He what? Where? I'll be right there. *(She stands up, she appears to be frustrated and angry. She looks at SANTIAGO.)* I'm sorry but I must go.

SANTIAGO: Why? What's wrong?

NEKIA: My son is in trouble; I have to go get him.

SANTIAGO: Would you like me to go with you?

NEKIA: No, but thanks anyway.

SANTIAGO: Can we reschedule? I would really like to get to know you better.

NEKIA: I would like to get to know you as well... Unfortunately, right now I don't have time to get to know anyone. I have to concentrate on the young man who already has my heart, no matter how bad he is!

SANTIAGO: <u>We</u> can focus on him *together*!

NEKIA: Santi you are so sweet, and I appreciate the offer. But you need someone who can give you the attention you definitely deserve! *(She smiles shyly.)* Right now I just don't have anything to offer you. I'm sorry, I must go. *(She hugs SANTIAGO and leaves abruptly. She's obviously torn between desire and responsibility.)*

Scene 2

NEKIA arrives at the music store "E-Drums." The manager meets her at the door.

MANAGER: Hello, Ms. Williams.

NEKIA: *(wary and agitated)* Hello. Where's Quincy?

MANAGER: He's waiting for you inside my office. I wanted to wait for you here to inform you of a few things. Your son wasn't the person who actually attempted to steal the CD. The culprits were his friends, Thomas and Lamont. I detained your son because I wanted you to know the kind of boys your son hangs around. It appears that your son knew nothing about his friends' agenda. I trust that my informing you of this will help you to take the appropriate measures. Believe me, the next time, and I hope there will be no next time, I will call the police! They won't care who was involved!

NEKIA: I understand. Thank you.

The MANAGER opens the door and QUINCY is sitting in the office frowning.

NEKIA: *(crossly)* Quincy, let's go!

QUINCY: But ma…

NEKIA: Quincy not now! I told you about hanging out with those boys. *(She pops QUINCY in the back of his head.)*

QUINCY: Ouch!

Blackout.

Scene 3

Simultaneously.

Lights up. We are in SANTIAGO'S living room. He's sitting on his couch thinking to himself and watching his phone. He picks up the phone and listens for the receiver. He remains seated and picks up the receiver again to see if his phone is dead. He then begins to sing, "Until You Come Back to Me (Stevie Wonder)." While singing he puts on his coat and he continues to sing until he reaches NEKIA'S house.

We are at NEKIA'S house. Without saying a word NEKIA gestures for QUINCY to go to his room. He walks to his room with his head down. NEKIA remains downstairs. She sits on the couch and puts her feet up on the table. She appears to be flustered. There's a knock at the door. NEKIA answers the door to find SANTIAGO standing there. They embrace as the scene ends.

Blackout.

Scene 4

We are in QUINCY'S room. He's sleeping in his bed. Suddenly his bed begins to rumble.

ALETHA: *(Loudly)* Wake up!

QUINCY'S bed rumbles again.

ALETHA: *(Louder)* Wake up!

QUINCY'S eyes open, he thinks he's dreaming. He closes his eyes and pulls the cover over his head. His bed begins to shake again causing him to fall out.

ALETHA: I said wake up!

QUINCY stands up alarmed.

QUINCY: Who is it?

ALETHA appears from the closet through a cloud of smoke.

ALETHA: Aletha Turner at your service! And boy do you need help!

QUINCY: *(shouting)* Mama! Mama!

ALETHA: *(slyly and slowly)* She can't hear you…

QUINCY: *(alarmed and frightened)* Who are you? What do you want?

ALETHA: No, the question here is who are <u>you</u>? An even better question is what do <u>you</u> want? In life that is...

QUINCY looks puzzled.

ALETHA: Now I'm sorry I knocked you out the bed. I hope you are ready now because we have a long trip ahead of us.

QUINCY stares at her quizzically. He's both angry and frightened.

QUINCY: Trip! What trip? *(with attitude)* I'm not going nowhere with you! Now, like I asked you before, *(stated slowly and sternly)* who are you?

ALETHA: Well I suppose we have enough time for a proper introduction. *(She begins to speak rapidly stating who she is in one breath.)* I am Aletha Turner, entrepreneur and former slave. I sold vegetables in DC and bought the freedom of many slaves and you Quincy... *(She takes a deep breath and begins again.)*

QUINCY remains quiet and afraid.

... are a child with no direction, who stresses out your loving mother. You act up in school, sleep on your potential, and hang out with kids who are going nowhere, all while insulting your ancestors who worked hard for you to afford your present liberties. *(She's out of breath.) (QUINCY puts his head down.)*

ALETHA calms herself and begins to speak normally. Before speaking she grabs Quincy's chin so he is facing her.

ALETHA: The ancestors elected me to bring you back with me. We have a message for you. Come on they're waiting!

QUINCY and ALETHA walk into the fog.

Scene 5

Lights up. We are in the Ancestors Inc. meeting room. There is a grand conference table in the room. In each chair sits an ancestor. ALETHA begins with introductions as she and QUINCY enter the room.

ALETHA: *(walking slowly and proudly)* Welcome to Ancestors Inc., the afterlife hangout of the African-Americans who helped shape the world you live in today!

QUINCY: Wow! This is amazing!

ALETHA: *(She stops walking. As she introduces QUINCY to the ANCESTORS, they greet him with a nod.))* Now over there we have Robert Bogle the "King of Catering." He worked his way up from a waiter until he led the most prominent catering business in the industry! And James Forten over there, he invented a device that made international trade more efficient by cutting the cost of transatlantic shipping. Imagine that! And James Boon over there, he started a construction company that could be outdone by no other!

QUINCY: Man, I've never heard of them before!

ALETHA continues to walk around the room with QUINCY.

ALETHA: Now you have your regulars that frequent Ancestors Inc. *(smiling)* like Dr. King, Marcus Garvey, Huey Newton, and Malcolm X, he's the CEO you know! Madame C.J. Walker, she always makes an entrance! And then you have little ole me. And you know what; it's not easy to get in this organization. You have to have worked hard to better the condition of our people in the U.S. and everywhere else if possible! I already told you a little about myself but here it is in depth… *(Slowly as if she's remembering her past. She looks off in the distance. Nina Simone's "Come Ye" plays softly..)* I was a slave. But I beat the odds. I challenged the system. I worked hard and I succeeded! I sold produce in Washington, D.C. to all the big whigs. *(She walks grasping her collar imitating her clients.)* And do you know what I did with my profit? I bought the freedom of slaves. Yep, I bought about one a year. Honey, I even had to purchase myself! Imagine that! I had to pay one thousand four hundred dollars for <u>my</u> freedom! Now that was a great discount because we both know I'm worth much more than that! *(ALETHA laughs and makes a proud stance.)* Huh, I bet those slaveholders in D.C. didn't know what they were investing in!

(ALETHA continues.)

Quincy honey, listen to me. *(QUINCY looks at her. He appears to be deeply affected by his experience thus far.)* You have to do what you've got to do to prosper, regardless of the circumstances. You are a part of a vast diaspora of Africans. People who look like you can be found almost everywhere! And you know what, because all you know is your "home far far away from home", you are going to have to work harder than everyone else to receive what God has in store for you. *(The ANCESTORS begin to gather around ALETHA and QUINCY.)* You must work hard for yourself first, and then you must consider all those who sacrificed for you like your parents and your <u>ancestors</u>! That's what's wrong with you kids these days! You don't know where you're going because no one teaches you about where you come from! Whoever said knowledge is power never lied!

By the end of her tirade all of the ANCESTORS have gathered around ALETHA and QUINCY.

ALETHA: Now we have a message for you so we're gonna try to deliver it in a way we think you'd understand. *(The ANCESTORS begin to dance to "Brotha" by Jill Scott." After watching a few moments, QUINCY joins them.)*

After the dance ends ALETHA continues.

ALETHA: So brotha, don't let no thing or no one hold you back! You got to just hang on. Q, come take a walk with me.

ALETHA begins to sing, "Someday We'll All Be Free" by Donny Hathaway. At this time she's walking QUINCY towards the door in which they entered. The door leads back to QUINCY'S bedroom. ALETHA tucks QUINCY in his bed while finishing the song. QUINCY, still under the impression that ALETHA and the ANCESTORS have been a long dream, shuts his eyes and falls asleep as QUINCY leaves his room.

Blackout.

Scene 6

Lights up. We are now in QUINCY'S room. He awakes to find himself in his bed. He looks at his watch and sees that he has overslept.

QUINCY: *(looking at his watch)* Man it's one o' clock! *(He gets out of his bed and stretches. He gets dressed then goes downstairs to find his mother sitting on the couch reading.)*

NEKIA: Well good afternoon! I was about to come upstairs and check on you! Are you okay?

QUINCY: I'm just fine Mama. *(He leans down and kisses her on the forehead.)*

NEKIA: *(with a puzzled look on her face)* Well, okay.

(The doorbell rings. QUINCY opens the door to find his friends.)

THOMAS: What up Q! *(They shake hands.)*

QUINCY: What up!

THOMAS: We're about to go hang downtown, you down?

QUINCY: Not today, I have some things I gotta do. Holla at me some other time!

THOMAS appears to be shocked and disappointed.

THOMAS: Well all right, see you around. P.

LAMONT: Alright Q.

QUINCY closes the front door and walks over to the couch to sit next to NEKIA. She seems to be surprised but delighted that QUINCY didn't leave with his friends.

NEKIA: Q, boy what's come over you?

QUINCY: Nothing… So Mama tell me about Daddy… How was he able to accomplish so much?

NEKIA: *(surprised)* Baby, your daddy set no limitations on himself. After he achieved one goal, he set out to achieve an even greater one. That's how we both wanted you to be. That's how you need to be! No boundaries, no self-destruction, no need in fighting yourself when there are other obstacles against you! Be proud but modest, be strong but compassionate, be yourself, be brilliant. Be an example of what once was. Don't live according to the world, live according to how it ought to be! But most of all, keep God in mind in all you do and you will <u>never</u> go wrong!

NEKIA begins to sing Donny Hathaway's "Someday We'll All Be Free beginning at the verse, "Keep on walking strong…" While NEKIA is singing the ANCESTORS are in the background providing backup singing. Towards the end of the song the ANCESTORS leave the stage. NEKIA and QUINCY remain on stage until the end of the song.

Blackout.

Scene 7

Lights up. QUINCY enters into the living room. He walks to the phone to make a phone call.

QUINCY: Terrence? What up? Yeah this is Q from down the street. Hey could you hook me up with some info about that young Black entrepreneurs program? *(He pauses for a second.)* No doubt, I'll be right there. P. *(QUINCY walks out the front door of his house. Jill Scott's "Brotha" reprise)*

Blackout.

The End

The Advent Of Planet Martyr

I am here to tell you this day October 1, 2001, that in the year 2200 the planet Mars will no longer be called Mars, but, will be renamed "Martyr."

In the year of two thousand two hundred Earth will be immensely overpopulated. Not only will habitable land be scarce; it will be nonexistent. By this time we will have discovered that yes; Mars is habitable. Yet, there will exist only one area of the planet where man can survive.

One dry and anomalous day in the year twenty-one ninety-nine, the leaders of each country on Earth assemble to brainstorm about a solution to this global problem of overpopulation. During the meeting, one of the delegates stands to address the representatives of the different nations saying, "Who are the people in the world who are not yet settled, who are preparing themselves to obtain a certificate of achievement to subsequently become productive citizens of the world?" While the representatives regard him with an air of indifference, the delegate shouts "students!" "I suggest that we send the graduating class of 2199 from all colleges, universities, and trade schools around the world to Mars with the objective of preparing Mars not only for themselves, but also for future inhabitants. After they have finished, we will send all people to Mars to live."

The representatives laugh for what seems to be an eternity. The meeting had begun three hours prior to this suggestion and they were in need of laughter to alleviate their unremitting boredom. When the representatives notice that the delegate is not participating in their hyena-like amusement, they hastily become silent. The delegate continues, "Earth can supply them with all the necessary resources for survival." One representative shouts, "Let's be practical here, this would never work!" "Mars has no electricity, therefore, they will have no light. There is nothing there but land; how will they survive?" Another representative stands, stating with the utmost conviction, "Survival of the fittest! Who could be better fit and what could be more powerful than fresh, brilliant, young minds? We really have no other choice, we have been here three hours already and all of our legal pads are blank!"

For some reason incomprehensible by humans of our time, the representatives will agree to the outlandish proposal of the exceedingly ambitious delegate. This agreement will change society as we know it.

When the graduates land on Mars the planet is completely dark. Strangely enough, even the moonlight refuses to reflect upon this area of the planet. For many weeks the premier "Martians" work in cooperation with each other, sharing resources to cultivate their land. Great friendships are built; each day the inhabitants live and work peacefully alongside each other. Though they are not able to see each other; their desire to fulfill their duty to their planet creates a common bond amongst all. Given that they are all goal-oriented, their conversations focus solely on the cultivation of their land. Even their names and topics such as religion and nationality are never discussed.

After three months without light, an electrical technician finds a source of electricity and subsequently there is light. When the light is provided the Martians are astonished by the sights before them. The light reveals all the work that has been completed up until that moment. There are striking temples, picturesque mosques, and astounding churches. The Martians finally see the people with whom they have formed binding relationships. They recognize and respect their differences but more importantly acknowledge that their divergence has converged to create a society paralleled by no other in the galaxy. The light also reveals that these people who have lived peacefully and worked together for a common purpose, represent many nations of our world; they are followers of many different religions, and all are of different shapes, sizes, and colors.

Three weeks before the arrival of the Earthmen, the Martians congregate to discuss all that must be completed before they arrive. During this meeting a Martian addresses the others stating, "I am not sure if you all realize this, but what we have achieved is a phenomenon. Okay, yes we did cultivate Mars! However this is not what I find to be phenomenal. We all shared a common bond, this bond made us closer, our respect for each other made us friends, and out of this respect came peace. We have a peaceful society! Those people on Earth could never understand how we cohabit. They were not here when we had no light and formed alliances ignorant of race, color, and religion." "When they come here, they will bring with them their ignorance, their airs of superiority over others, and all the other negative conceptions that plague Earth. We must not let them alter our society, our way of life! I suggest that we call down to Earth and let them know that they must find somewhere else for those people. We will just have to explain our position to them."

So the Martians call to Earth and explain their position to them. Earth of course is displeased with this pose. The governments in turn threaten to cease the provision of resources to Mars. The Martians reply, "keep your resources, your threat only fortifies our stance, reminding us of your ignorance and cruelty!"

The Martians stand by their decision to refuse entry to the people of the planet Earth, thus the governments of the planet Earth cease to provide resources to the Martians. The Martians continue to live without resources for four months following the Earth's embargo. Unfortunately, by the end of the year two thousand two hundred, all of the Martians die of starvation. When the land of the Martians is explored after the death of the last Martian, many diaries are found.

An excerpt from one of the diaries reads, "Though it will be short-lived, knowing that it is possible to live in peace and harmony amongst many different people is enough to quell all the hunger pains in the galaxy. I've been starving for peace all my life; at least this craving has been fulfilled." This excerpt from the diary will be published in a book entitled, Remnants from Mars. The people of planet Earth will read this book and realize what the Martians died for. It is then that the name of Planet Mars will be changed to Planet Martyr, commemorating those who died for unity and serenity.

The End
Of Life As We Know It.

About The Author

Veronica Nicole Chapman is a graduate of Spelman College. She is Founder and CEO of Boxxout Enterprises. She is also a linguist and world traveler. She resides in New Jersey.

www.ingramcontent.com/pod-product-compliance
Lightning Source LLC
Chambersburg PA
CBHW020403290526
45785CB00005B/2419